# Gifted
# Game Designers

Heather C. Hudak

Checkerboard
Library

An Imprint of Abdo Publishing
abdopublishing.com

# ABDOPUBLISHING.COM

Published by Abdo Publishing, a division of ABDO, PO Box 398166, Minneapolis, Minnesota 55439. Copyright © 2019 by Abdo Consulting Group, Inc. International copyrights reserved in all countries. No part of this book may be reproduced in any form without written permission from the publisher. Checkerboard Library™ is a trademark and logo of Abdo Publishing.

Printed in the United States of America, North Mankato, Minnesota
052018
092018

THIS BOOK CONTAINS
RECYCLED MATERIALS

Design: Kelly Doudna, Mighty Media, Inc.
Production: Mighty Media, Inc.
Editor: Liz Salzmann
Cover Photographs: iStockphoto (left), Shutterstock (right)
Interior Photographs: Alamy, p. 13; BagoGames/Flickr, pp. 23, 29 (top); Courtesy MIT Museum, p. 17; Division of Medicine & Science, National Museum of American History, Smithsonian Institution, p. 18; iStockphoto, pp. 4, 7, 9, 10, 15, 25; Jeff Keyzer/Flickr, pp. 21, 28; Shutterstock, pp. 27, 29 (bottom)

Library of Congress Control Number: 2017961589

**Publisher's Cataloging-in-Publication Data**
Name: Hudak, Heather C., author.
Title:  Gifted game designers / by Heather C. Hudak.
Description: Minneapolis, Minnesota : Abdo Publishing, 2019. | Series: It's a digital
    world! | Includes online resources and index.
Identifiers: ISBN 9781532115332 (lib.bdg.) | ISBN 9781532156052 (ebook)
Subjects: LCSH:  Video game designers--Juvenile literature. | Video games--Design--
    Juvenile literature. | Occupations--Careers--Jobs--Juvenile literature.
Classification: DDC 794.8--dc23

# CONTENTS

Get Your Game On. . . . . . . . . . . . . . . . . . . . . . . . . . . .5

Getting in the Game . . . . . . . . . . . . . . . . . . . . . . . .6

Game Designer Jobs . . . . . . . . . . . . . . . . . . . . . .8

Bringing a Game to Life . . . . . . . . . . . . . . . . . .12

Programs at Play . . . . . . . . . . . . . . . . . . . . . .14

Early Computer Games . . . . . . . . . . . . . . . . . .16

From Arcade to Home . . . . . . . . . . . . . . . . . . .20

Computer Revolution . . . . . . . . . . . . . . . . . . .22

Game-Changing Moves . . . . . . . . . . . . . . . . . .24

Timeline . . . . . . . . . . . . . . . . . . . . . . . . . . . .28

Glossary . . . . . . . . . . . . . . . . . . . . . . . . . . . .30

Online Resources . . . . . . . . . . . . . . . . . . . . . . 31

Index . . . . . . . . . . . . . . . . . . . . . . . . . . . . .32

4

# GET YOUR GAME ON

**Do you enjoy playing video games?** Perhaps you like to build new lands in Minecraft or LEGO Worlds. You can go on exciting adventures, fight bad guys, and test your survival skills. There are no limits to what you can do!

Maybe you prefer sports games such as Pro Evolution Soccer or Madden NFL. You can pick your favorite teams to play against and even create your own players. If you enjoy solving puzzles and fighting monsters, Legend of Zelda, Knack, or Super Mario Odyssey might be for you.

Game designers create the video games you love to play. Some designers create games for desktop computers. Others make games for **mobile** devices such as smartphones or tablets. They may also design products to use on game consoles, such as PlayStation or Xbox. Game designers create fun and exciting worlds where people of all ages can play.

# CHAPTER 1
# GETTING IN THE GAME

**Game designers come up with storylines, characters, settings, and rules for video games.** They plan all of the details. This includes the number of levels, the menu options, and the way the controllers work with the game.

Most game designers are creative. They have big imaginations. Some are writers. They come up with plots for games. They write words for characters to speak or text to show on screen. Game designers are also artists. They draw characters and **environments**.

Being creative is just one feature of a good game designer. Game designers have solid **technical** skills too. They can use different types of **software**. They know how to use **graphic** design programs and write computer **code**. Game designers also know a lot about different types of **hardware**, such as desktop computers, game consoles, and **mobile** devices.

Designers create video games through scripting and coding. The code is processed by software to produce commands, events, and characters in the video game.

Most game designers were game players first. They love gaming and know what features make games fun to play. But designing video games isn't just about having fun. It's serious business too.

# CHAPTER 2

# GAME DESIGNER JOBS

**Most game designers work for video game development companies.** Three of the biggest game companies today are Nintendo, Rockstar Games, and Electronic Arts. These companies employ hundreds of people to design, program, and **market** their games.

Not all game designers work for one company. Some are freelancers. Game companies may hire freelancers to work on specific games. When a freelancer's work on a project is done, he or she moves on to a different company or project.

There are also independent game designers. Independent designers create and market their own games. They may try to sell their games to large game companies to produce. Or if an independent designer's game becomes popular, a game company may offer to purchase it.

Most game designers have many different skills. This includes writing, drawing, computer programming, and more.

Game designers must understand how to build all parts of a game. However, they often **specialize** in certain areas of game design.

Game designers usually work in teams made up of designers who have different specialties. A lead designer is in charge of the team. This person makes sure each part of the project fits

Nintendo has created popular video games like Mario Kart and consoles like the Wii and Switch.

Successful video games showcase graphics and new technologies as well as appeal to consumers' interests.

together to create the finished game. The lead designer keeps a detailed calendar and budget for the project.

Creative roles include **scriptwriter**, artist, and sound engineer. The scriptwriter writes the stories and **dialogue** for the game. The artist creates the game's **graphics**. These include the backgrounds, characters, and scoreboards. The sound engineer chooses the music, sound effects, characters' voices, and spoken instructions for the game.

More **technical** roles include the programmer and the game testers. The programmer writes the computer program for the game. He or she combines the writing, **graphics**, and sound to create the game.

The game tester does just that. He or she tests the game's programming for any mistakes or problems. The game tester also makes sure the instructions within the game are clear, so users will know how to play it.

All of the team members work closely together. They each make sure their part goes with the others. For example, the **scriptwriter** might include a barking dog in the game's story. The artist will then need to know to design a dog character. And the sound engineer will need to find or record the sound of a dog barking.

Game designers should have good communication skills. Being able to explain ideas clearly and listen to others' ideas helps the team members work together smoothly. This is important because a team may work together for months or years to develop a new game.

# CHAPTER 3

# BRINGING A GAME TO LIFE

**The first step in game design is coming up with the basic idea.** Some designers think of their own ideas. Others work for companies that decide what games to develop. Once the idea is chosen, the next step is creating a game design document.

The game design document describes how the game will work and what it will look like. The document may have character sketches and descriptions, game **scripts**, and more. The game design document lists every action and feature of the game and how it will be played.

The design document also includes a storyboard. The storyboard shows all of the scenes that will be in the game. It includes drawings for each character, setting, and prop. Each scene is placed in the order it will appear in the game.

As the designers complete the design document, they create a prototype of the game. A prototype is a small sample of the actual game. It shows the types of **graphics**, interactions, and

**Video game testing is extremely important. These tests may result in thousands of changes throughout the creation of one game.**

details that will be used in the full game. It's a way to see how the final game might look.

As the game is being fully developed, it goes through a lot of testing. The game's development team will include game testers. Many game companies hire additional game testers as well. Game testers play the game and report any problems or bugs they find. It can take a lot of people to make sure there are no bugs in the game.

# CHAPTER 4
# PROGRAMS AT PLAY

**All game programmers need to know computer programming, or coding.** There are many programming languages to use in coding. C++, Java, Python, and HTML5 are some of the most common languages used by game designers.

Programmers can also use **software** packages specifically for creating video games. Examples include Unity, Game Maker, RPG Toolkit, and Adventure Game Studio. These packages have **templates** that game designers can use for their own stories and artwork. The software often has built-in testing tools as well.

Game artists or **graphic** designers often use programs such as 3ds Max to create **3-D** artwork for their games. This may include characters, buildings, props, scenery, and more. Designers use **animation** programs such as Maya and Blender to bring the 3-D art to life. This adds motion to characters and objects. SketchBook and Adobe Photoshop are other programs game designers use for creating artwork and animations.

Video game designers are often skilled artists. They draw
characters, objects, and backgrounds that fit together.

Sound is an important part of most video games. Some
games have music that plays in the background. Most also
have sound effects, such as car engines or nature sounds.
Sound engineers know how to record and edit sound. They use
programs such as Pro Tools to prepare sounds for games.

**Technology** is always changing and improving. New
computers and devices become **available**. New programs and
languages are constantly being developed. Game designers need
to keep up with these changes.

# CHAPTER 5
# EARLY COMPUTER GAMES

**Computer games have come a long way since the first one was created in the 1950s.** At the time, computers were just starting to be developed. They weren't advanced enough to handle many different programs, such as games. So, early computer games ran on their own machines.

In the 1950s, Cambridge University student Alexander Douglas designed a machine for playing tic-tac-toe. The game was called OXO. Players used a **rotary**-dial phone to enter their moves. Over the next few years, other computer scientists and researchers designed computer games. These included electronic tennis, chess, and card games.

These early games were not widely **available**. Some could only be played on one specific computer. The main purpose of the games was to show what the computers could do. Few people other than the computer scientists and researchers who developed the games played them.

In 1962, computer scientists at MIT, including Dan Edwards (*left*) and Peter Samson (*right*) made improvements to Spacewar!

Then, in 1961, American computer scientist Steve Russell created Spacewar! at the Massachusetts Institute of **Technology** (MIT). Players used controllers to move spaceships around and shoot **missiles**. At first, this game was played mainly by researchers and university students.

However, by this time universities had developed larger computer systems. Spacewar! was very popular and spread across computer systems at many universities. Because it

The Brown Box had some features that video game consoles still have today. These include controllers and the ability to play multiple games. Paper cards were used to program the different games.

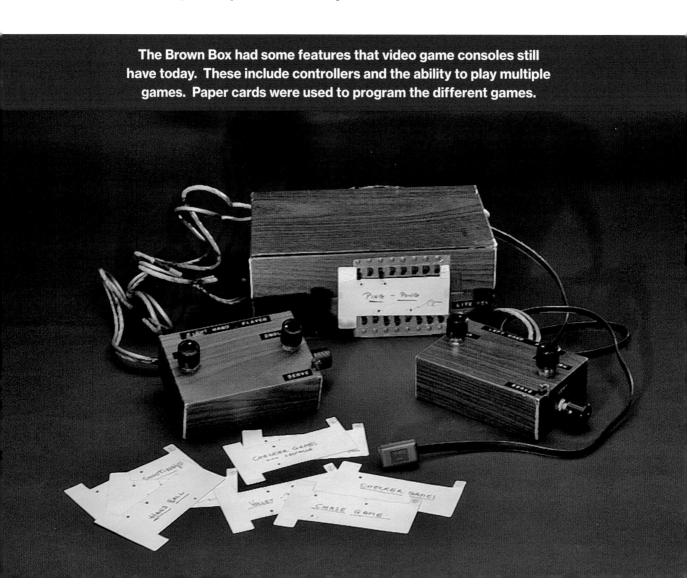

was the first game to be widely played, many people consider Spacewar! to be the first official video game.

While universities and research institutions in the 1960s had computers, very few people had one at home. But television had become very widespread. Most households had at least one TV. In the 1960s, TV engineer Ralph Baer developed a new gaming device. It would allow games to be played on a TV screen.

Baer completed his device in 1968. It was called the Brown Box. The Brown Box could be connected to a television. It included simple games such as ping-pong and checkers. The Brown Box was never manufactured for sale, but **technology** company Magnavox bought Baer's idea. In May 1972, Magnavox released the first home video game system. It was called Magnavox Odyssey and was based on Baer's Brown Box device.

Unfortunately, the Magnavox Odyssey did not sell well. One reason was that many people thought it could only be used with Magnavox TVs. This was not true, but Magnavox wasn't able to make Odyssey successful. Only about 350,000 Odyssey consoles sold between 1972 and 1975, when Magnavox stopped producing it. But that was not the end of the home gaming system.

# CHAPTER 6
# FROM ARCADE TO HOME

**The Atari video game company was founded the same year Magnavox released Odyssey.** It focused on video games for public places such as **arcades**. Atari's first game was based on the Odyssey's tennis game. Atari called its game Pong.

Pong came out in November 1972. In the game, players move paddles up and down on the screen to hit a ball. The game could be found in arcades, restaurants, and malls across the United States. Throughout the 1970s, Atari and other video game companies produced many video games. Video game arcades opened to provide people with places to play these games.

In 1975, Atari created a home TV **version** of the Pong arcade game. It was sold in Sears department stores. People would wait in line for hours to buy it. Two years later, Atari released its 2600 Video Computer System (VCS). Unlike the Pong game, the Atari 2600 could play many different games. Each game was on its own **cartridge** which could be **inserted** into the game console.

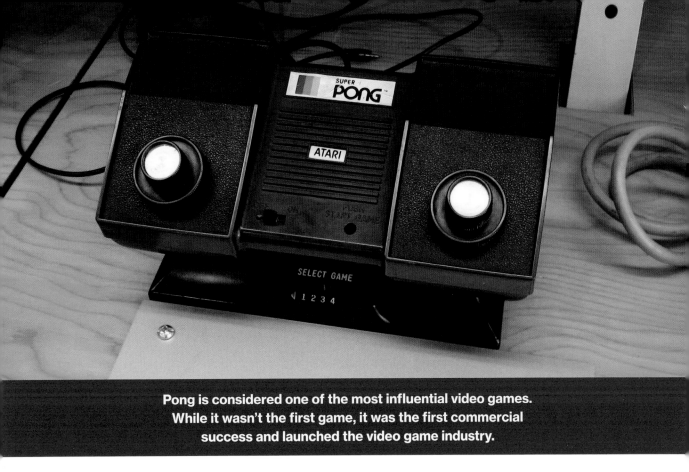

**Pong is considered one of the most influential video games. While it wasn't the first game, it was the first commercial success and launched the video game industry.**

Over the next few years, more and more companies began building video games for use on game consoles. The Nintendo Entertainment System launched in Japan in July 1983. The same year, SEGA released the SG-1000. Both were very successful. But game consoles soon faced competition from the home computer.

# CHAPTER 7
# COMPUTER REVOLUTION

**By the 1980s, more households had home computers.** This opened up new doors for video game designers. In 1980, Microsoft founder Bill Gates designed the world's first personal computer (PC) game. It was called DONKEY.BAS. Players steered cars around donkeys on a road. DONKEY.BAS was a simple game that other computer companies poked fun at. Still, it inspired game designers to come up with new games for computers.

In 1993, the internet became publicly **available**. Over time, more and more people used it for business, socializing, and entertainment. **Online** computer games became popular around the world. By the late 1990s, game designers were making massive multiplayer online games (MMOGs).

Thousands of people **subscribed** to MMOGs. Popular games included Ultima Online, EverQuest, and World of Warcraft. Online communities began to form around multiplayer games. Gamers formed groups to talk about and play their favorite games.

The Dreamcast was the last video game console sold by SEGA in the United States. It was discontinued in 2001.

In 2000, SEGA released Dreamcast. It was the first successful internet-ready game console. Users could connect to the internet through the console and play games on their TVs. They didn't need to have computers. Dreamcast paved the way for other **online** gaming consoles such as Microsoft Xbox, Nintendo Wii, and Sony PlayStation.

Over the next few years, online gaming exploded. Online stores opened for people to purchase internet games. By 2015, more than 1.5 billion people around the world were using the internet to play video games.

# CHAPTER 8

# GAME-CHANGING MOVES

**The way games are created has changed a lot over the years.** A major shift happened in the mid-2000s with the release of smartphones and other **mobile** devices. These devices have smaller screens and less memory than computers and TVs. This provided new challenges for game designers. They had to figure out how to make the games look good without being slow.

One of the first companies to create a popular smartphone game was Rovio Entertainment. In December 2009, the company released Angry Birds. In the game, players control a flock of birds who need to rescue their eggs from hungry pigs. The game quickly became a huge hit. By May 2011, it had been **downloaded** 200 million times. By 2017, there were several **versions** of the game. All together, they were downloaded 3.7 billion times.

Live streaming has also changed computer gaming. Live streaming is posting videos **online** as they are being recorded.

Virtual reality video games can be used in education.  Games exist that allow players to look at art, study the human body, and explore landmarks.

Computer game players can stream their games on video sites such as YouTube as they play.  Then other gamers can watch the games being played and post comments.  This helps build large game-playing communities.

Some of the latest games use virtual reality (VR) or **augmented** reality (AR).  VR uses **3-D** artwork to create artificial **environments**. These **technologies** require players to wear special headsets.

Game designers use VR to make players feel like they are a part of the game. Players move around inside the gaming world. They interact with objects and other players inside the game. For example, in a VR baseball game, players could feel like they were actually playing in big-league games. They could hit home runs and catch fly balls.

With AR, game designers can make **3-D** images appear in the player's real world. They can use AR to add sights and sounds to a real environment. When done well, the player cannot tell that some parts of their surroundings aren't real.

These are just a few of the technology advancements that are shaping video game design. Who knows what the future will bring? But it is undeniable that the video game industry is a huge business. It is worth about $100 billion worldwide. Nearly 65 percent of households own a gaming device.

One thing we can count on is that video games are here to stay. Gamers continually look for new games and challenges. Game designers who have exciting new ideas will be an important part of the future of gaming.

In 2014, **software** company Niantic wanted to create a game using Google Maps **online** mapping **technology**.  At the time, Nintendo's video and trading card game Pokémon was extremely popular.  In the game, players collect different characters called Pokémon.  Niantic partnered with Nintendo and The Pokémon Company to create Pokémon GO.

Pokémon GO uses a form of AR to bring Pokémon characters to life.  Players use Google Maps to look for Pokémon near their location in the real world.  When they find Pokémon, they appear on their smartphone screen.  Players can also view Pokémon through their phone's camera.  It looks like the Pokémon are right in front of the players in the real world!

Pokémon GO caused a **craze** when it was released in July 2016. It was **downloaded** 130 million times in the first month!  By June 2017, the game had been downloaded more than 750 million times.

# TIMELINE

**1950s**
Alexander Douglas designs the game OXO.

**1975**
Atari produces a TV game console for playing Pong.

**1961**
Steve Russell creates Spacewar!

**1968**
Ralph Baer completes the Brown Box.

**1972**
Magnavox releases Magnavox Odyssey.

## 1983
Nintendo and SEGA release home gaming consoles that can play multiple games.

## 2000
SEGA releases Dreamcast.

## 1993
The internet becomes publicly available. People start playing computer games online.

## 2009
Rovio Entertainment launches Angry Birds.

## 2016
Pokémon GO is released.

# GLOSSARY

**animation**–a process involving a projected series of drawings that appear to move due to slight changes in each drawing.

**arcade**–an amusement center where people play coin-operated games.

**augmented**–made greater, larger, or more complete.

**available**–able to be had or used.

**cartridge**–a case or container that you put into a machine to make it work.

**code**–a set of instructions for a computer. Writing code is called coding.

**craze**–something that is very popular, often for a short time.

**dialogue**–a written conversation between two or more characters.

**download**–to transfer data from a computer network to a single computer or device.

**environment**–surroundings.

**graphic**–of or relating to visual arts such as painting and photography.

**graphics**–pictures or images on the screen of a computer, smartphone, or other device.

**hardware**–the physical parts of a computer.

**insert**–to put in or into.

**market**–to advertise or promote something so people will want to buy it.

**missile**–a weapon that is thrown or projected to hit a target.

**mobile**–capable of moving or being moved.

**online** –connected to the internet.

**rotary**–turning around a central point like a wheel.

**script**–the written words and directions used to put on a play, movie, or television show.  A person who writes scripts is a scriptwriter.

**software**–the written programs used to operate a computer.

**specialize**–to pursue one type of work, called a specialty.

**subscribe**–to agree to receive a publication and pay for it if it is not offered for free.

**technology** (tehk-NAH-luh-jee)–machinery and equipment developed for practical purposes using scientific principles and engineering.  Something related to technology is technical.

**template**–a computer document that has the basic format of something and that can be used many different times.

**3-D**–three-dimensional.  Having three dimensions, such as length, width, and height.  Something that is three-dimensional appears to have depth.

**version**–a different form or type of an original.

ONLINE
RESOURCES

**Booklinks**
NONFICTION NETWORK
FREE! ONLINE NONFICTION RESOURCES

To learn more about video game design, visit **abdobooklinks.com**.  These links are routinely monitored and updated to provide the most current information available.

# INDEX

animation programs, 14
arcades, 20
artists, 6, 8, 10, 11
Atari, 20
augmented reality, 25, 26, 27

Baer, Ralph, 19
Brown Box, 19

characters, 6, 10, 11, 12, 14, 27
computer programming, 6, 8, 11, 14
computer scientists, 16, 17
creativity, 6

DONKEY.BAS, 22
Douglas, Alexander, 16

Electronic Arts, 8

game consoles, 5, 6, 19, 20, 21, 23
game design software, 14
Gates, Bill, 22

Google Maps, 27
graphics, 6, 10, 11, 12

home computers, 21, 22, 24

internet, 22, 23, 24, 25

live streaming, 24, 25

Magnavox, 19, 20
Microsoft, 22, 23
Minecraft, 5
mobile devices, 5, 6, 24, 27
multiplayer online games, 22

Niantic, 27
Nintendo, 8, 21, 23, 27

online gaming, 22, 23, 24, 25

planning, 6, 12
PlayStation, 5, 23
Pokémon Company, 27
Pro Tools, 15

Rockstar Games, 8
Rovio Entertainment, 24
Russell, Steve, 17

Sears, 20
SEGA, 21, 23
smartphones, 5, 24, 27
Sony, 23
sound, 10, 11, 15
storylines, 6, 10, 12, 14

televisions, 19, 20, 23, 24
testing, 11, 13

universities, 16, 17, 18, 19

virtual reality, 25, 26

Wii, 23
writing, 6, 8, 10, 11

Xbox, 5, 23

YouTube, 25